Momentary Thoughts

Timeless Letters, or as you'll have it.

Also by Torry Fountinhead

The 7 Pillars Your Authentic Self Stands On, Part I of The Essential Companion Series

The Beauty, Part of The Contemplation Series

The Soul's Openner, Part II of The Contemplation Series

Shush! It's a Secret, The Lake Hides His Dummy, Part of The Rainbow of Life's Secrets

Poem: Good Enough, Part of Forever Spoken, The International Library of Poetry

A Tip of an Iceberg Meditations, a series of short books

and many more at work…

Momentary Thoughts

Timeless Letters, or as you'll have it.

Part II of "A Tip of an Iceberg Meditations" Series

By

Torry Fountinhead

Airé Libré Publishing & Computing Ltd.

Print ISBNs:
ISBN-10: 0-9781499-9-8
ISBN-13: 978-0-9781499-9-4

eBook ISBNs:
ISBN-10: 0-9808964-1-X
ISBN-13: 978-0-9808964-1-1

© 2014 Torry Fountinhead
All Rights of this work are Reserved. No part or whole may be used, copied or reproduced, stored in retrieval systems, or transmitted, in any form or by any means whatsoever, including electronic media, mechanical, photocopying, recording, or otherwise.

For more information contact:
Airé Libré Publishing & Computing Ltd.
Suite 306, 185-911 Yates St.
Victoria BC V8V 4Y9 Canada
Tel: 1-250-592-3099.
http://www.al.bc.ca   info@al.bc.ca

Book Web-Site URLs:
http://momentarythoughts.atipofanicebergmeditations.ca

Part of:
Http://www.atipofanicebergmeditations.ca
Http://www.tipofaniceberg.ca
Http://www.atipofanicebergmeditations.com
Http://www.tipofaniceberg.com

Table of Content

Momentary Thoughts	i
Momentary Thoughts	iii
Table of Content	iv
Momentary Thoughts	viii
Prologue	1
Navigating the Journey of Life	3
Enjoying the Now	5
Clarity and Focus	7
Focus, as the tool to understand the Now	9
Duality & Narrow Perceptions	11
Half-Full Glass and Celebrations	13
Is Your Plate Full?	15
What is the Common Denominator?	17
The First Ingredient	19
Celebrations and The Soul	21
Time Elusiveness	23
The Value We Know We Have	25
Constriction vs. Restriction	28
Your Life's Journal and Title	30
The Inner Compass Needle	32
When a Non-Movement is an Hibernation	34
A Thought for my missed Tuesday	36
Reflective Morning	38
Silence is Golden	40
Revealing the Hidden	42
In Private versus In the Open	44

Multiple Instants	46
Navigating the Imagination	48
Conscious Action vs. Unconscious One	50
A Hope	52
Happiness: Re-Examine What Generates It for You	54
Early Morning Music On My Mind	57
To Blog or Not to Blog	59
Getting a Relief vs. Rests	61
The Tree of Secret Blessings	64
Talents, Free Will, Fruition, and Abundance	67
New Gifts versus Gifts as Conceived	69
Discrepancy Between The Outside & Inner	72
What About Shining Light On and On	75
Crossing The New Year's Line	77
Think Small? In A Deed	79
Aspires and Inspires	81
Visual Input Impression and Our Lives	83
The Zeros In Our Lives	86
Impressions	89
Creation Like Water	90
A Word About This Series	93
Notes	95-100

*How hidden, yet revealed daily,
is the wisdom of the ages.*

Momentary Thoughts

Timeless Letters, or as you'll have it.

Prologue

At first, you might notice that each entry is titled, but they were not addressing any particular recipient, yet, you may distinctly feel that they were written with someone in mind, and you'd be right.

Like all self-expressions, the need to talk, whether in speech or in writing, occurs in response to Life itself, and the way it touches us - Humans.

A thought is created - and captured, herein.

Essays may be developed, but sometimes – keeping it short may create a far greater engagement with you, the reader, than spelling it all out.

How wonderful contemplation may be – if we just take the time…

Momentary Thoughts

Navigating the Journey of Life

While hiking on our path in life, the terrain changes and affords us the wonderful variety of mountains, hills, valleys and canyons.

Each one of them represents a different view and vantage point, none more important than the other – all are needed.

The mountains afford us a visionary vantage view point where, the far reaching vista of our lives and paths seem clearer and apparent.

The hills afford us a chance to pause, a reprieve from our daily toil.

While the peaks of our mountains allow us to feel 'on top', they also accentuate the fact that we are 'alone' up there. The peaks could be more barren than the valleys, and in reality their greater power is in enabling us to have a higher view of where we're going to, and where we are.

The valleys, on the other hand, are mostly lush and rich – having the resources needed for our move forward. Actually, only the valleys – the ground level, are continuous, allowing us to move forward. Imagine us leaping in the air from one

Momentary Thoughts

mountain–top to the next...

Therefore, although we are attracted to the mountain–top and value it more, it is the hiking through the valley that makes it possible – allows us our own individual expression to have the greater power, and Live.

We need to speak more of it, reframing our understanding and definitions, and creating the winning mindset for our respectful journeys.

Enjoying the Now

Enjoyment of the present moment can only be felt if you are focusing on this moment thus, let go of past memories and future concerns before you take another step.

Talking about steps, one of the very good lessons learnt in Tai-Chi is that unless you know where you stand, you cannot be stable. Once you're stable, you may look ahead. The key is to know how to focus.

The power of your breathe; for example, can only be harvested in the present moment. You cannot utilize the past breathing, nor the future ones. You do have to carry on breathing well, if you want to carry on living – and this living is exactly denoting on your 'current' power, and none other.

The same principal is valid with regards to what it is that you focus upon 'in' your life. Whether it is your ability to 'smell the roses', or 'feel the fresh breeze', or your ability to 'be inspired with your creations', your focus may be likened to a sharp or blunt knife, which one do you need to perform your 'operation'?

We do need to contemplate more on it,

garnering the power of a centered mind that helps in the Right way to focus.

Clarity and Focus

Did you experiment, in your childhood, with directing the sun light through a magnifying glass on a piece of a paper? Did it set fire?

Well, then you've brought into clarity the sun rays by focusing them through the glass. The sun rays, as such, do not set fire on their own unless, they are brought into focus.

Our mind is so very similar, while scattered – it has no significance, and while focused – it gains clarity and becomes ingenious.

I'm not suggesting that people will only be single-faceted rather, that while your plate is full of demands, tasks, chores etc. that you will 'decide' to concentrate on one thing at the time, because while concentrating – you're creating focus, which brings clarity, which allows your mind to be more discerning and inventive. You're then able to complete the task in a much better way and in a shorter time span.

Not only have you completed what was within your responsibility, you're now entitled to the feeling of accomplishment, as well as all the benefits of the learning that took place, and the Kudos.

In our lives, we are bombarded by so much information, interference and demands, seen or unseen, that we land up being easily overwhelmed, so let us take the reins and decide the course and speed that we are to proceed with life, we are entitled to.

Life is work nonetheless, it is not slavery.

Focus, as the tool to understand the Now

Let's use the analogy of binoculars. While looking through them, we narrow our field of vision, because we're concentrating on the object of our interest. At that time, our mind is engaged solely (or nearly so) with that object, an example would be bird watching.

While using this ability of focusing in the present time, we can isolate each feeling that we feel, each sensation – or anything that we perceive either from our physical senses, or ideas and thoughts from our mind.

The advantage of becoming aware of the 'parts' that comprise our present feelings is the ability to relate to each part.

Only by acknowledging what we feel right now, whether we know why we feel it or not, can we have the power of doing anything about it, if we so chose to.

Our sensations and feelings are our inbuilt indicator mechanism, our own tool, to be used to our advantage, and not to be at the mercy of.

A wise person is a person, who through

all of theirs' experiences, managed to learn about Life and themselves.

Do you know that the difference between a wise person and a clever one is that the wise person will not fall into the trap that the clever person will find a way out of?

A wise person, in addition, will also slow down their responses, so to choose the right way to respond, and certainly not to react.

First give yourself the permission to feel. Next, acknowledge your feelings, and with tender love and care, attend to them. Bless your ability to feel – it is a mark of a person who's alive. It is your energy, your power, and your tool – put it to good use.

If ever you do get overwhelmed, remember, a conglomeration of feelings will always feel and look ominous therefore, pay attention to each one separately, acknowledge each one, and so you may have the power to transform them, with the intent of resolving them.

Paying attention to your surroundings will also allow you to discern what needs to change.

Your power to act exists right now, at every moment. Isn't this wonderful?

Duality & Narrow Perceptions

In many of the books, and other material, I've read through the years, I came across this belief system called Duality. I've been given many examples starting from Night & Day, Good & Bad, Right & Wrong, or even Life & Death.

I remember my childhood bewilderment, not understanding what the adults were talking about, I couldn't see the sharp differentiation they referred to, I only saw continuation. I thank my more mature age for seeing the truth.

Creation and our Universe work in cycles; the best example would be the tide of the sea. There are no just a 'tide in' and 'tide out' statuses, but the whole flow of the tide *coming in* and *going out*.

In the same way, while the Earth is rotating around the sun, we have a flow of light in different quantities, and the beautiful seasonal changes. I cherish each one of the statuses.

Tongue in cheek question would be: what is the opposite of 'right'? You would be correct in both cases if you choose to answer 'wrong' or 'left'!

If you look around, you would see that everything is part of a cycle. You cannot just relate to the pinnacle points in that cycle, as it is like a circle, with no start point, nor end. Even Life and Death are just appearances, as there is no loss in Creation. Everything is going through a transformation, all values remain.

I do believe that if Human-Beings would relate better to the cycles, our lives will be better in every way.

The importance of wellbeing is dependent upon it.

Half-Full Glass and Celebrations

Today, in a celebratory mood for a couple of personal reasons, I looked at Life – yet again.

It always amazes me to notice how, despite Life's peculiarities, being in a celebratory mood makes it look possible.

You see, while you are able to recognize value – the half-full part of the glass, you're able to engage in appreciation. While in appreciation, your mind may only recognize 'like' things, so Life seem possible then, rather than challenging and hard.

Who are we to know for sure what will come next. Who are we to limit, with Human-like belief-systems, what Life's tide may bring into our lives.

Surely, when you're thirsty you will see the half-full part of the glass and drink it to quench your thirst, and not complain that the half-empty part of the glass is empty, without drinking a drop.

Acknowledge value in your life and appreciate it. Use it as your ladder's rungs to better your life. Climb from one moment of appreciation and value recognition to another, as you set forth in life, and look forward to its best.

Well-Being is built of moment by moment wellness, make sure you utilize each moment.

Is Your Plate Full?

Maybe you feel overwhelmed, or maybe you feel like screaming, but have you thought to look at your 'plate of life' lately?

Life's plate, many times like a plate of food, is the definition of what you, as a regular Human-Being, are capable of handling at the same time. Although we are unlimited in principal, we do need to 'take it in stride'.

In the same way even an heavy-weight lifter would have a limit, but may train himself to take on a little bit more at a time – again only to a certain degree defined by his own body, you are 'handling' Life's weights in your everyday demands.

So what can you do if you feel overwhelmed, frustrated, or any other negative emotion?

What about pausing at first, taking a deep breath, and looking at what you have on hand, not in relation to the immediate 'demand', but as part of all the demands bearing on you at that moment. You see, the total sum of the weight comprises the total sum of your Life's demands.

Imagine that you have reached a 'certain'

limit, not necessarily one that you may not surpass, but one that might ask you to further 'train' before you carry it together with all the rest. Therefore, no blame is necessary, no giving up, nor any other loss.

It will be very helpful to have lists of 'musts', 'would like to', 'empowering activities', and 'better done than not', as example of categorizing your Life's demands. It will make life more lovely if you choose from all lists versus doing just the 'musts', because your nourishment will be then more harmonious.

This is yet another step towards Well-Being, and your commitment to a good life depends on you handling well what is on your plate.

What is the Common Denominator?

The common denominator to what? You ask.

Well, what is that attribute that is part of the following actions: waiting for something to transpire, watching a flower bloom, watching a tree bearing fruit, watching the sunset, watching your children grow up, focusing on a task while what you're doing is unfolding, waiting for a letter, and so on…

The required attribute for you to be able to do all of the above, plus more, is *patience.*

Patience stands for: endurance, tolerance, persistence, fortitude, serenity, perseverance, forbearance, and imperturbability.

Patience is actually born deep within us, if we are just willing to wait for it to bubble up. Unfortunately, most times we allow our emotions to be like the moving sea, raging and toppling over anything in its way. Our poor beloveds don't have a chance.

Patience is tied up to our breath; the more we are aware of it, the more we're connected to it source of power within us. For patience to bubble up, you just have to pause and breathe.

There are many gifts in its wake, if we just allow patience to be part of our lives. If we exercise all its facets namely, endurance, tolerance, persistence, fortitude, serenity, perseverance, forbearance, and imperturbability, we would find that life can be lived far more easily, surrounded by people who aren't afraid of us, and whom might help us to have a far more fruitful life.

You might ask, but what about the other people we're exposed to, who are not patient? We, too, must exercise patience's attributes while remembering that their outrage is an emotion that will pass quicker, if we just don't feed it the fuel of arguments. Tolerance does mean accepting others, as they are, and not trying to force people to be, or do, what you think is best. No wars would have been necessary if people could be more accepting.

The gifts of patience are many, and the most important one is peace. Peace is the best ground to bear the fruits of creation.

The First Ingredient

The first ingredient necessary for any action and to live life to the fullest is *Willingness*.

This is why breathing is designed to be involuntary.

Many people, given the choice, would, at some time or other in their lives, give up and stop life therefore, breathing is involuntary. One really has to go to a great extent to stop it, as well as have outstanding determination to do so.

In coming back to willingness, it's quite apparent that unless we are willing to participate in life, we may be robots at best.

When we have willingness, Life becomes a dance whereby, our inspiration and passion propel us forward, and help us to climb the ladder of achievement.

Willingness is tied to our innate growth-ability therefore, it requires far less amounts of energy in order to activate it. We'll find many more ways, ideas, and joy if we'll perform all in our lives with willingness.

One of the important keys in life is to have the Right-perspective. The Right-perspective lets you see that there are options open to you, there is hope, you can keep on going being optimistic, without being delusional. What seems to be your gloomy reality can be looked at, as just one more stepping stone to move from to a better reality.

Willingness also enriches you with the feeling that you do have a choice that you can be the navigator of your life; you have the power to say what will be in your life, and for how long.

It is the pleasure and beauty in Life that you are opening yourself to. It is your chance to shine, to whatever extent, and who is to say how.

An axiom may be set to say that you are here therefore, you were born. You are therefore, allowed to 'be', 'choose', 'succeed', regardless of what other people say. Your own mind is yours to use.

If anything, be willing to live life, and see, step by step, moment by moment, how you may do it best.

Cheers for your Good Life.

Celebrations and The Soul

Like a fresh breeze, gently caressing your face, like cool clear water quenching your thirst, like a swim in a fresh lake on a hot day, so (and more) is a celebration to the soul.

On this Canada day, we all have a reason to celebrate regardless, what is the state of your mind, or health. Take a moment and forget the cares of the world, they will undoubtedly manage without you for one day.

Any celebration, may it be Canada Day, your birthday, or even a smile a baby smiled sweetly at you, are all portals for joy and happiness, directly entering your soul, the joy – I mean, not associated ego's pain to the occasion.

In the same way the idiom "The Beauty is in the eye of the Beholder", joy, too, is your own capability of perceiving it and allowing it in, you do need to be conscious for it though.

The Pharaohs, as an example, built huge pyramids, all stocked with many goods, food, jewellery, and the like, because they believed that on the way to the heavens, and on arrival, they would need it all, both to consume, as well as to denote on their status, but look what happened.

Neither a rich king, nor pauper, takes any physical goods with them, when they pass on from our beloved Earth. The only thing that lasts is that which we enrich our soul with, and joy, love and happiness are those intangibles.

Life ordeals do not, in any way, have the right to rob you of any moment of joy and happiness therefore, be conscious, recognize the occasions, and open those portals to your soul - allow your soul to be enriched, it will serve you better in the long run.

May your celebrations be plenty, and your sorrows few.

Time Elusiveness

If it wasn't for the cyclical nature of Earth, we wouldn't have experienced neither day and night, nor the demand of tiredness – sleep.

Thus, we invented the notion of time, and its measurer – the clock.

We all know that time is relative namely, regardless of the elapsed number of minutes; our feelings measure it in accordance with its content, and not its length.

The issue arises when the tasks and activities to be performed in a single day over exceed our ability to comply. May it be due to bodily or mind tiredness, or any other reason, it is simply a fact that some things cannot be performed on a specific day.

If we're lucky, we may still do it and proved it to be 'better late than never' alas, sometimes we just have to let it go, and declare our loss.

How are we to remain content regardless of the outcome?

Firstly, we do have to detach ourselves from the outcome, when we're still in the stages of pre-due time.

Secondly, try our best to do that which is Right, Just, and Good, as first priority while, remembering to take care of our survival.

Thirdly, re-assess our priorities, as the day progresses, and not just stream along with disregard.

Lastly, embark on a life devoid of guilt and blame. We can only use life's experiences as yard sticks to measure our assumptions and choices, and try and learn from it and do better next time.

Each day is a new opportunity, each day is a promise of a new start, and each day is glorious – if you dare to declare it so.

Would you declare it so?

The Value We Know We Have

An interesting situation with Human-Beings is that they perceive their own value alas, not always the right one.

We continuously measure ourselves against one another, as well as figures from literature, arts, history, and storytelling. This measuring may generate arrogance as well as meekness, joy as well as misery, self-confidence as well as fear.

Many a times, we forget that most things on Earth are relative, and our value is no exception. Even an interesting quote from the Bible illustrates it, referring to thousands of years ago opinion, "…And there we saw the giants, the sons of Anak, [which come] of the giants: and we were in our own sight as grasshoppers, and so we were in their sight." (Numbers 13:33 KJ)

How can we see ourselves as 'grasshoppers' and expect another to see us as a giant?!

It would have been a respectful, polite, and correct assumption to make that each one of us has got a value, whether seen or unseen, whether acknowledged or unacknowledged. Even a weed is called a weed, and only said to be an herb after people recognized its value.

The value installed in us is not necessarily valuable in every situation, for every person, therefore, it is imperative to find the place and audience to whom we may bring our value and thus, benefit them and ourselves in that process.

At the same time, we should not become desponded just because someone doesn't value us. After all, a vegetarian will not appreciate a chef's best creation of Beef Stroganoff.

We should develop a collection of reference points to indicate to us our 'home' location. The location in time and space, which will be a moving target as we develop and grow, that we are able to contribute positively to Life.

It is self-doubt that we have to eradicate from our conscious view of ourselves, because we are not in the position of truly understanding fully our value, our viewpoint is too near.

Agreeing that each of us has an important value, that we are like a flower destined to bloom in full glory, if we just find the right soil, and environment to live in, will contribute to our well-being, as well as the well-being of all around us.

The saying 'Know Thy Self' is not a cliché, but a necessity.

Good Luck, as you embark on this adventurous journey.

Constriction vs. Restriction

Imagine this: you are gasping for air, your breathing mechanism is working fine, but somehow – there is not enough air, or maybe oxygen. The result might be a negative kind of feeling that might be named in many names, but it will certainly propel you to action; uncover your face, open the window, anything that might bring to you fresh breathable air.

In exactly the same way, if your limbs are held tight, and you're not able to do anything for yourself – a prisoner of a kind, the same negative feeling will inspire you, and will create an urge for action in you , not always possible, but it will be created.

These examples are physical examples of constriction. Alas, constriction is not limited to the physical. Mental and emotional constrictions are actually far more common place, and extremely damaging.

Restriction on the other hand, reminds me trimming of a rose bush, so it will give more flowers, or pruning of a fruit tree, again for it to produce more fruit.

Restriction, if applied correctly, will

actually focus the flow, so that we're almost becoming like a pipe, with a straight forward ability to let the stream of our expressions, creativity, and being, be more focused, intentful, devoid of as many distractions as possible – like a laser beam.

When you can breathe freely, when your Spirit can envisage your dreams, even when you keep the details of it for yourself and not share it with others, when you are continuously invigorated by your expectation of its manifestation in your life, know that your apply restriction – and it is positive.

If you feel deflated, confused, full of anxiety, worries, hard of breathing, lost inspiration, and practically ready to 'jump the boat', know that you're constricted, and look immediately for the way out.

Freedom – is our right; the freedom to choose – is our responsibility; easily flowing with the river of life – is our joy.

How about listing all that you feel and finding out if you're constricted, or have applied healthy restriction upon yourself.

Momentary Thoughts

Your Life's Journal and Title

It is well known among authors and writers that the two most important items to start writing with are a journal and a good title.

I would like to use this as a metaphor for our lives.

What if the history of our lives is the story written in the journal of our memories?

Could we decide on a title for the story of our lives, or are we to continue with the 'apparent' title that was thrust upon us by our initial environment and youth's experiences?

Does the title have to be permanent, or may we set an overall theme with different chapter titles?

I am sure that you can see where I am going with this. Our lives are multi-faceted; we have many chapters in it, as well as the ability to close or open a new chapter at any time.

How about if the 'book' (Life) title would be something along the lines of "The Greatest Person I Can Be", and then – each chapter will have its own sub-title.

How about if the current chapter's title

will be changed to "Finding and Aligning with my True Self Now"?

Let the wisdom of Life teach us that we are pliable and thus, are able to re-create ourselves and our lives to satisfy a higher level of excellence, joy, and fulfilment.

I must say that I enjoy working with people on this self-re-invention.

The Inner Compass Needle

Have you ever thought about the innate ability of the compass needle to point to North regardless, where in the world you're standing?

Of course, we could explain it in physics and other sciences, but the fact remains that it does so. Even if the poles were to change polarity, the pointing of the needle will still exist.

We are in bodies, which being flesh and blood, electric currents and magnetism, are also subject to the laws of Physics, so might it be that we, too, have an inner compass needle? Only it does not have to point to North, it could point to our own north.

Can we then ask the question what would our own north be?

I do sincerely believe that each one of us is entirely unique; therefore, one might say that each one of us will have their own unique north.

Could it be that we were endowed with a unique mission, which act like a magnetic pole that attracts our inner compass needle?

I think and believe that the answer is – Yes.

Therefore, let us listen within. Let us develop the trust in our abilities to hear and decipher what we hear. Let us bring forth the faith that we can, as well as fuel our drive.

Courage, after all, is knowing what needs to be done, and do it regardless, whether we are afraid, doubtful, or lack in any way.

When a Non-Movement is a Hibernation

Hibernation, as the womb of manifestation, is an unseen state. The cocoon of the caterpillar does not reveal the transformation process, only the end result of a beautiful butterfly.

How are we to live through a non-movement state in our lives while, it is an unknown. How we to distinguish whether there is a transformation process taking place to reveal a marvellous transformation, or is it just a dead-end, requiring us to turn around and find the main road again.

It seems to me that at certain times, we do all that there is to do, regarding a certain subject and yet, nothing is showing whether it is right, or not.

At other times, we don't even complete all that there is to do, and the outcome already shows itself in the whole of its magnificence.

Does the subject of time has anything to do with it (again?!), as it states that "all has its season...", or are we bound by the collective "instant results" belief system?

Here is the place, and time, that we must stay connected to our true self, to our true purpose (and not somebody else's), and draw the strength from it to be our inner staff, to stand steadfast in our belief in ourselves, and the fact that we are all unique, all special, all the apple of the eye of Creation.

There is a lot to say for daily solitude moments, you may call it meditation, or you can call it your inner-space-time where, quietude will allow for re-alignment – becoming congruent with your inner self, in a cool, calm, and collected manner.

What secrets does your soul reveal to you? While you let go of ALL self-judgement and belittling.

A Thought for my missed Tuesday

You may have noticed that last Tuesday I didn't write my regular weekly blog, and for a good reason too.

In addition to my beloved general Internet and PC audience, I also wanted to share my blog with the Mac / Apple based audience and therefore, I created an equivalent iTunes podcasts for my blog entries (you may find it in iTunes if you just search for Experiential Elixir), and now regardless of which computer / tablet / phone you're using, you may access it freely.

Writing, unless it comes from the heart, it is just a scribbling. The same is true if you're trying to write from the heart while, your mind is in its analytical frame, as per the needs for composing 'code' versus 'prose'.

Now, a week later, I'm picking my writing back and hoping that you're there to read it.

In the old days, when people used to correspond, writing letters by hand, they had to take a special time with no disturbances, when they would look within, and not only compose the content of the letter, but also its presentation, spelling, style and such.

This moment of solitude afforded them true connection to their heart and their inner rhythm, so much so that it, in itself, granted them a sense of accomplishment.

I am sure you're aware of the vast difference to this day's writing, so let's slow down, look within, connect with your addressee, and share a moment of heart's delight.

I enjoy in your enjoyment of reading my blog / podcast, and always amazed at how vast a field my audience is. Our Earth, our globe, is indeed one large village.

Reflective Morning

What is required, you should know. What is right, you should also know.

In the morning, fresh off sleep, even if you don't know what the day may bring, or even if you're already somewhat anxious about the day (s) ahead, take a moment for yourself.

A moment granted for your own quite reflection, may just render you the best inspiration for a better day.

You see, it is in the quite of the morning, when all is yet undecided that a reflective frame of mind can reveal to you both, what you're worried about, as well as what you could be grateful for. It can show you the multitude of responses / reactions possible; it can help you to distinguish what would be the Right choice.

Sometimes, a reflective morning may enhance in you the ability to see that the cyclical nature of time is calling you to observe, absorb, listen, and be soft and pliable – adaptable for the best outcome.

Mornings are blessings, as they allow us to change our outlook on Life, change our attitude to a more appropriate one, change our actions –

if so necessary.

The morning is a promise, which is entirely tide up to our view of Life. Let it be then, positive, calm, cool, and collected. Let it be the fountainhead of new ideas, possibilities and solutions.

Let it be gentle.

May your day ahead be blessed with all that is good for all.

Silence is Golden

Did you ever stammer when silence was actually required? Did you ever hear the saying "a picture is worth a thousand words"?

I would like to present it in a different way that might seem complex, but it isn't.

Communication, between any two beings, is done on many levels, of which the base of it all is the total frequency emitting of each one.

Human-Beings are of many facets e.g. The Soul, the individual's emotional history and current state, the individual's belief systems, opinion, conditioning, apprehensions, the individual physical state and comfort, etc.

There are a number of frequencies that operate at the time, but they are conveyed in a 'mean frequency', which therefore would be, at first glance, general or vague at best. Almost like trying to listen to the radio between two stations.

To our aid comes the silence. When we allow silence to enter the picture, we invariably create a certain calm, which in turn allows the other party to 'collect themselves' and thus, be more homogenetic.

At the same time we, ourselves, enter our calm as well. While at a calmer state, one is capable, consciously and sub-consciously, to discern far more information from all the frequencies – vibrations one receives, knowingly or unknowingly.

Consequently while silence is respectful etc. it is also a very good tool, and sometimes just save the situation. It is also an aid to focusing with ease.

Silence may also grant you, and the other, that moment of privacy, which the Western society does not put that much value in; they prefer that you would 'answer immediately'.

The privacy silence grants you is far more comprehensive than described here, each one of us has an ocean vastness within that we may not even be able to traverse in one lifetime.

Give silence the chance to endow you with its riches.

Revealing the Hidden

Both in Jeremiah and in Psalms, there is a reference to the difference between Human-Beings and idols whereby, it says: "...eyes have they, but they see not..."

Alas, even we the Human-Beings are not always able to see that which is hidden, that which is veiled under our level of understanding or belief.

When the pilgrims to the ancient temple of Apollo in Delphi saw the maxim "Know Thyself", they knew that without acknowledging their own power of understanding (or lack thereof), their survival will be questioned.

I would like to attract our attention to that that we are evolving beings. For our highest good, we should perform self-enquiry on daily basis, enough to make sure that we may walk the day with a sure-foot, as well as consider the morrow.

We need to look for patterns that appear in our lives that might clue us in to an underlining cause, which brings forth the effects of life. Of course, when the effects are good – we can repeat these patterns, but when the effect rob us of a good life – looking at them and researching to find the hidden Truth underneath, as well as take the necessary actions, may save our lives in the end.

Suffering is not the innate condition of Life, but the result of us not living Life in the Right Way. A marshal-art artist may be free of hurts after a battle, due to their ability to move in the Right Way, and so we too can do in Life.

We must never be afraid to ask and look for clarity. We must never postpone taking care of ourselves, so we will not deteriorate to a point of no return.

We can heal ourselves in every moment of life; even if we 'think' that it is too late. Our nature is to strive, grow, evolve, develop, and fill ourselves with true Joy.

May we succeed in doing so.

In Private versus In the Open

These days, our lives are so much in the open – in public where, we do not have the time or space to conduct almost anything in private.

Even our thoughts, opinions, and tastes are constantly being influenced by the media, teachers, and others, and we thought that at least our thoughts will be our own.

I would like to invite you to exercise your power of choice – your birth-right. Choose what is to be kept private – away from the public eye, not because you feel ashamed, or guilty, but because you would like to cherish it, savour it without the need to neither justify yourself, nor diminish it by trying to explain it to someone, who might have different tastes in life.

Many authors of great books actually found their way to writing, not because they were afraid of public speaking, but just because they wanted to birth their self-expression in private, be it as they wished to be – with no disturbance, judgements, and then send it to the world 'as is'.

Imagine how much more creative each of us could be, if we would have the time and the privacy of our own mind to conjure and bring forth ideas, dreams, and even acknowledge inner joy.

That which is considered 'input' , may it be in noise, food, ideas, or anything else, has to be received, processed and assimilated, we cannot just be constantly in a 'receiving mode', we must have the time and space to assimilate that which we 'received' already.

Our mind is our great gift, the basis with which we can express our creativity, our ability to be a contributing Human-Being within our societies. Our mind asks us for a 'time off' where, we give it privacy, it can then come up with wonderful things.

Try it, you'd be surprised.

Multiple Instants

Watching a program on Knowledge Network, about Emily Carr, the great painter from Victoria on Vancouver Island, BC Canada, I was amazed that she wrote "… How could we ever draw and paint the west coast with its multitude of sceneries and vastness…"

I drew comparison between the wonderful sceneries, and multitude and vastness of the landscapes, to the multitude of moments in Life.

Each moment in Life is utterly unique and special, inspiring us to 'paint' our lives in vividness and exuberance, if we just allow it to be so.

Anywhere on Vancouver Island, wherever you walk, sail, or fly over, the sceneries are so wonderful and changing that an artist can spend their all life painting every corner, and never run out of subjects, and/or inspiration.

The same applies to Life.

Can we dare relate to our lives as canvases to be drawn upon? We may have as many canvases as we wish, and as many paints too; we are not limited in any way whatsoever.

The greater question would actually be, can we dare relating to each moment of our lives, as a new canvas, and make new choices yet again?

It is in our ability to exercise our power of choice, together with a good dose of optimism, that we might create wonderful lives for ourselves.

Let us have the faith in the hidden Goodness, and reveal it in the creation of our own lives.

Navigating the Imagination

In my Momentary Thought titled ***'Navigating the Journey of Life'***, I spoke about navigating the actual terrain of our lives. Yet, we need to speak about a preliminary requirement, a very important one, in my humble opinion.

We firstly live in our minds. In our minds we have information, which is derived of many sources, e.g., our personal lives concerns and joys, our work life, our country's situation – political and otherwise, and more.

To these we have to add the 'added semi-realities', which we are fed with via all forms of media, whether real or fiction, our friends, neighbours, other countries etc.

If you would to sit and watch, as an observer, the 'screen' of your imagination, you'd be surprised as to how the 'personal' and the 'other' realities intermingle, and how your own emotions and feelings actually derived out of both.

We seem not to compartmentalize our mind. We seem to have a free-flowing river of information. Alas, if we want to navigate our own lives, we really have to only deal with that which is our own.

If we understand that the mind is mostly operating in associative fashion, we may forgive ourselves for having our thoughts flow from a subject that is in the forefront of our mind, to a similar theme from a movie, or the news.

It is OK to enjoy the flow if you're just day-dreaming, but if you're trying to 'deal' with the issues of your own life; you must separate that which is 'your own'.

Once you do that, you may firstly feel relief that your burden is not that large. Secondly, you may priorities the issues with ease.

Our imagination is 'wild', because we are 'natural creators', and as such we take a lot of input to help our creation. Alas, it is in the clarity and focus that we may actually create eventually.

Slowing down, taking time for yourself, allowing yourself the pleasure of day-dreaming, as well as knowing when to stop, and concentrate at what is at-hand, will allow you to take yourself lightly while, you take life correctly.

Conscious Action vs. Unconscious One

Like a fish in the sea, with every flip of its fin or tail, it moves here or there, we determine the direction of our movement in life with our actions, big, or small, kind, or not.

The more important key to our actions is whether we act consciously, or not.

You most probably heard of the term 'auto-pilot' well, we too might act in rote, meaning, we might be acting out of habits, conditioning, or fears, without an intentful thought behind our actions.

Taking responsibility in life mostly means that you recognize your freedom to take actions, as many times, and in many ways, as you wish, and then learn from the presented results. Taking a conscious-action mostly means that you are able to measure yourself and your actions in reference to the desired outcome. When adjustment is needed, you adjust your view and take a better action.

Taking an unconscious-action is like being adrift at sea, and many a times at the mercy of the elements and the environment.

This is why it is helpful to have a purpose / mission / goal in life. Your purpose is used then as the destination, which is not set in stone, nor that you're obliged to keep it so for the rest of your life. When the destination is clearer, it is far easier to set a course and therefore, the required actions.

Conscious-action is easier to execute when the destination is known, but when it doesn't, you could always have a general 'theme' for all your actions, something like: "an action which is in line with my highest-good and the highest-good of all", this way you at least know that you're not on the way to harm yourself, or another.

Our actions determine where we are in life, as well as where we going to. Don't you rather know where you're heading to?

We can always talk about how to have a better clarity in life, so our actions are well thought of.

A Hope

Have you ever heard of the story of Pandora an her box, from the Greek Mythology? Well, it is a good story to read that has number of good points to learn from, but the one I would like to refer to here has to do with the content of the box.

It is said that when Pandora opened her box, all the evils of the world came out of it and filled the world. The known Human history has definitely demonstrated that.

Yet, the box contained one more thing, ONE more thing – Hope.

Evidently, hope, in the story and our history, is the most powerful weapon. Hope can help us all to steadfastly stand in the face of all evil. Hope offers the alternative, which leads to growth, empowerment, and development.

Hope lead the way to evolution while, all else can stunt it.

Life is about evolving to a higher level, developing and becoming more. Joy is our sustaining energy while, we're on our way of our growth. Hope is the innate force that propels us to want to grow. This is why abusers try to stunt the hope within others, but it is our responsibility to always maintain a strong hope – it is our birth right.

A small, but powerful, book that delves into it in depth is *Man's Search for Meaning* by *Viktor E. Frankl.*

Now, the testament for Hope's power is in the mere fact that it was the only positive thing in Pandora's Box, and it remained in the box, awaiting Pandora's recognition of it.

We, too, must recognize the meaning and power of Hope. If we will, we will also recognize our 'Right' to live, and live well.

Each one of us was created uniquely. Each one of us is a prism, of a different sort, there to reflect the Light, without us – the world would not be the same.

Let Hope help us strive for the best in us and Life.

Happiness: Re-Examine What Generates It for You

We all want to be happy. Happiness seems to be the state where we feel powerful and content, at the same time.

Although a lot has been written about happiness, there is one point that I'd like to bring forth, and it is about what *we actually believe that will make us happy*.

I don't necessarily mean to say: spiritual versus material, or any other definition, but for what each one of us actually define, for ourselves, will make us happy.

Happiness may be momentary or long lasting, profound and deep, or quickly evaporating.

If we would be positioned at the outcome, and look back at our yearning and expectations, would we still feel happy with the results, or would we ask ourselves: why did we actually want that specific outcome (or thing, or someone, or state).

Imagine that every time we 'think' someone, something, or anything will 'make' us happy, we would consciously position our 'honest' imagination at the outcome (when we actually achieved it), and look if it does bring us happiness, which type of happiness, and at what price.

If the happiness lasts for an hour, and then we feel that it is was *not enough*, shouldn't we ask if we might have made a 'definition error'?

Tongue in cheek question: If one of the items you optimally wish for is happiness in self-independence in transportation – transportation-freedom, would you set your happiness at getting *only* a 5 ton truck or a vehicle that can really answer your life-style needs?! Can you imagine doing your grocery shopping with a 5 ton truck? (Good-luck with the parking...)

In the same manner, any definition may be re-examined and made more probable to fit the kind of life we want to live.

If you could paint the picture of the life you want to live, re-examine each part, as to what extent of happiness it will really bring you, and then set-up your expectations – you might just get the life you yearn for.

Alas, we should repeat this re-examination regularly, because we grow, evolve, change in taste – and not only in age and abilities, so for our lives to be good – we must flow with the flow.

We are unlimited beings, capable of greatness and therefore, we should be prepared to reach for a life that is for our highest good, and may I add: the highest good of all.

Make sure though, that your re-examination is done compassionately, and free of judgement.

May your life be Good, as you flow in Life's cycles.

Early Morning Music On My Mind

I love music so much, well, not all types of music, but many. You can imagine then that many a times, my expression would be connected to music.

In the mornings, those after an adequate sleep, my soul commune with me in song. The other morning I woke up to singing in my mind the "…Blue skies smiling at me, nothing but blue skies do I see…" song.

I was looking forward to another glorious day, when I discovered that the day was overcast, and even drizzling here and there. On looking out the window, another song came into my mind – "…On a day like today…" that Pat Boon used to sing.

You know very well that it is pretty hard to control the weather, but I was determined to have a glorious day, so instead of dampening my mood – I thought of Gene Kelly "Dancing in the rain…", and actually went out to enjoy the day.

While being happy with the day 'as is', the day cleared within the hour, and a glorious blue skies and sun shine commenced to be for the rest of the day.

Was the morning song about blue skies a prophecy? Or was it an indication of my state of mind.

Did it matter to me that the weather changed after all? Yes and No.

You see if the state of mind is to make of the day a glorious one, so you shall, but the opposite it true too. You can make a day miserable – as easy.

I count myself blessed that I have music running in my veins, as well as in my mind.

Whatever is that which is special to you, cherish it, develop it, and respond to it.

Your days may be as blessed as you allow them to be regardless, of what is going on, at least because not all is under our control, nor are we always successful in trying.

Later on, I remembered that Pat Boon's song name was "letters in the sand", and laughed that actually each day can be renewed, as easily as the sea washes the sand clear.

To Blog or Not to Blog

To Blog or Not to Blog – that is the question, or is it?

In days gone by, before TV and other modes of singular occupation, people would sit and share in a conversation, or any other mutual activity like singing or dancing.

These days, we try to find the closeness of a conversation in other ways – one of which is a blog.

I imagine myself as a traveller, dropping-in for a visit, engaging myself in a conversation with you, before being on my way again.

Like a chance meeting in a store, or some other place where, we might just have a few minutes to chat – to me blogging is one way to achieve the same.

They say an author, or writer should be in touch with their readers, but seeing that I am firstly a Human-Being, I'll engage in a conversation first. If I had your address, I might have sent you a hand-written letter, written with my fountain pen.

I wanted to say that, in my part of the

world, we had a gorgeous day today. The skies were so blue, the sun shown warmly although, the air was crisp. I was in a celebratory mood despite the fact that tomorrow is Remembrance Day – or maybe because of it.

I am full of thanks and appreciation for the best life we can have today, helped by so many of our dear ones, who perished in previous (and current) wars, by the important intent, that life is worth living and cherishing.

In respecting the many that perished, let us appreciate today with all its gifts.

Take a moment to acknowledge your breathe, your day, your family and friends, the cloths on your back, the changing of seasons, the greatness of Life, Live in this moment, and love it ALL.

Getting a Relief vs. Rests

It could be that you're exhausted, overwhelmed, had enough, and any other multitude of definitions that portray the situation of being depleted. This, you know, may lead to numerous symptoms, behaviours, and loss of self-belief and control.

Let's take a moment (before you rush to either a 'numbing' agent, or a doctor of any sort), and have a look at some simple definitions.

Any rope, if it could speak that is, would tell you that it will wear down if you carry on pulling it so tight. We, too, have an inner rope, but more than this – we have a brilliant mind, which is to be exercised here.

When a situation is re-occurring, what we need is a relief versus a rest. You see, you might need the rest right now, but you will not benefit from it if your issue carries on as-is.

A relief is felt after you apply a solution to a problem, when you know that the issue is now resolved.

If you take a rest after you resolved the issue, and felt the relief, your whole-being is going to truly rest and thus, rejuvenate.

You might not always have the right tools, skills, or gifts to find a solution, but the mindset that is looking for the solution is a different mindset than the one who is focused on the problem.

Our nervous system is not built for a continuous and unrelenting challenge, and our mind may 'spring' into a solution if we just give it the 'moment' it needs.

Many people were in similar situations, and many of them also wrote books, courses, and such, to share their learnt wisdom with others. We don't 'always' have to re-invent the wheel (so to speak), or do it by ourselves. We could consult (or read) others, and focus on finding the specific solution that will bring the desired relief.

Believe that a solution exists for any 'problem', 'issue', or anything you might not have the full understanding for. Believe that you might not see it right now, but if you just let go, and allow your mind to have its moment to exercise its brilliance, you might be pleasantly surprised at how fun it is.

It might take a short time, or long, patience is required, and this is the reason I used the word moment – as it is an undefined length of time.

    Good Luck, and we may talk some more.

The Tree of Secret Blessings

A thought had occurred to me, pertaining to trees. Watching a beautiful tree, outside my window, as its leaves turn to gold during this season, it looked as if all its leaves were gold coins hanging there for all to see their luster.

This tree reminded me of the Frankincense tree, the *Boswellia sacra,* of which the Frankincense is taken from.

I would like to compare the tree to a Human-Being, on a specific point, as a species comparison. Forgive my generality, as I would like to remain in the metaphor realm, there's the place where the message is.

The actual Frankincense is a dried tree sap, and in order to get it, the people make cuts with a very sharp knife along the bark of the tree, in effect, injuring it, so it may release the sap – its salve of healing. They then leave it to dry, and collect it the next day.

The tree is left as is, and its innate tendency for healing allows it to re-grow the bark, only to be met with yet another slashing. The people, on the other hand, actually trade it for thousands of years, and throughout the world.

You see, Frankincense has both ritualistic and healing properties.

Imagine us, the Human-beings, if we could adopt this tree's behaviour namely, each time we're injured, instead of lashing out at others, or at ourselves, we would immediately release a healing balm – to heal ourselves and bless others.

We are beings that have feelings, our Humanity is measured by its ability to feel and have emotions, why not then employ this ability to our advantage versus destruction?

Would you like to try something else? Next time you're hurt, for any reason, imagine that your feelings are a healing sap, which is there firstly to heal yourself and your wound, as well as trigger re-growth, and then imagine this sap extends to become a blessing for others. The Frankincense tree didn't distinguish who's going to benefit from it, it gave it freely.

A very good thing can come out of this test, firstly, you'll minimize your ability to get hurt and by that give power to others who hurt you, and secondly, your 'blessings' could be your loving and compassionate self-expression to the world, which could be in any endeavour, and bring true joy.

Momentary Thoughts

It is too tiring to live a life of resentment, resistance, grudges, and any other negative emotions. Let us turn our lives around, and get to be the great beings we were created to be.

All The Best For The Holidays.

Talents, Free Will, Fruition, and Abundance

How many shades of green have you seen in nature?

How many talents do people have?

Choice is the key to Free will, and so multiple occurrences of talents are required in order to make a choice.

Like the diamond ability to reflect so many colours only after it's cut with so many facets, so are we shining our talents, as the occasion may rise in our lives.

A tree gives of its fruits, as per the type of the tree it is, we are gifted to give multiple types of fruits, and we may choose to give one type, like Mozart, or multiple types, as we wish.

Have you ever asked yourself what joy could be from actually using anyone of our talents and gifts? At the same time making sure that we do not use them just because we have them, but use them when they make us feel empowered and joyful.

Imagine the destination you would like to reach in Life. Ask what would be the characteristics of the person who will succeed in reaching that destination, make a comparison with your own talents, gifts, and skills, and see what you would need to add, so you may reach the desired destination.

You may also imagine yourself as a fruitful tree, ask yourself what fruits you would like to produce, and repeat the same comparison, as above.

The mere fact that each one of us has multiple talents, gifts, and skills denote that we're versatile. We're open to exercise our choice making, and even change our minds, when it helps us grow and become a greater version of ourselves. There is no limit, only the one we hold in our own minds.

Let's experience a life of freedom and self-expression, bringing good to the world, and our fellow beings. Life can be so wonderful when we allow it to be so.

New Gifts versus Gifts as Conceived

We are blessed with many gifts yet, we do need to decipher the difference between them, in order to understand their value and impact.

The 'gifts' we are born with actually, from the moment of our conception, are abilities that can open for us wonderful windows in life and bring us great joy, or even cause us some sorrow at certain times. These gifts are for us to use, both for our own benefit, as well as benefiting others.

Although, as a word of caution, don't always believe that all gifts are to manifest to their full fruition, some remain as buds – forever ready to bloom, even if they don't bloom, but never lost.

Another type of 'gifts' is those gifts bestowed on us by the wisdom of the ages, and the wisdom of sages (hidden or known) that live around us. This wisdom is like singular pearl that is dropped by us at a moment of need – it can bring revelation, solace, change of heart, and many other things. You may collect those pearls to have as your own string of pearls to be shared with others, as the case may be.

A third type of 'gifts' is the one derived out of our own experiences, when you internalise an experience and grow from it, when you then own it, and may use it again and again (the gift, not the experience.)

There is a saying that asks: "what is the difference between a wise person and a smart one?" and it goes to answer: "a wise person will not fall into the trap that a smart person will find a way out of…"

In the same way, our experiences in life teach us, and give us the opportunity to learn. These learnings become our Life Gifts.

You may have noticed that I only related to non-material gifts, the reason being that even a material gift carries with it a non-material value, which is incredibly important, like, generosity, care, love, sharing, friendship, charity, and many other values held in their intent.

Therefore, you may see how rich we are – gift-wise, and how important it is for us to actually acknowledge, the source, value, and existence of a gift. How else are we to 'know' that Life is a Gift?

In this season of giving, 'give' your acknowledgement for someone else's natural gifts, 'give' gifts of your own experience, and 'give' any other gifts inclusive of the Right Intent packed with them.

Discrepancy Between The Outside & Inner

It is the Holidays Season, so many wonderful holidays, and reasons to celebrate; suddenly came upon us in rapid succession.

Sometimes, we may feel that we were caught by surprise, the year is drawing to conclusion so quickly, and we didn't have time to prepare. We scurry to oblige ourselves, our families and friends, and even our employers, and cannot find a moment of reprieve – to take a breath – and adjust.

Well, we forgot. We forgot that time is only a symbolic marker for our cyclical life. We forgot that the holidays are trying to help us remember moments of significance whereby, instead of life being routine and dreary, life offers us windows of opportunity to experience something deeper, and more rewarding. This is also in spite of the background non-positive and alarming news of all that is transpiring in the world.

Regular build-up of exhaustion, fatigue, irritation, and the like, may cause us to feel on the verge of explosion – where we would have to take a breath, we would have to pause. At the same time, we're supposed to feel the joy already, and participate in a light-hearted manner.

What if we don't feel like doing so? What if our inner-being is not adjusting that quickly, is not ready to rejoice, and actually might even feel guilty because of it. After all, in reality, there is a lot for us to be thankful for.

Let us remember that we are beings that need rest, regular deep breathing and self-nourishment before we can attend to the outside. Let us remember that if we do not take care of ourselves, we would not be there, in any case, to participate in the rejoicing.

You can enjoy a celebration while being entirely quiet, as much as you can do it while singing from the top of your voice. Who is to say what is better?

The key is to have an open heart, sound mind and body, and strength, and be present, so you may be able to make the choice of sharing in the joy.

If you find that you cannot take advantage of these windows of opportunity right now, remember that another opportunity will come. If you doubt that they will, make a point to create them yourself, after all, you are entitled to declare an occasion joyful, if you do indeed feel the joy within you – even for a moment.

May your heart will open to feel joy, love, and goodness, with every breath, every moment, and every day of your life. May they be plenty, as the dew drops of every morning.

What About Shining Light On and On

The Holidays Season bring us many things, and not in the least Light and Joy. We're all surrounded by music to remind us of it, decoration lights, candle lights, and the business of remembering loved ones by sending cards and buying gifts, and of course the planning of a getting together to raise our glasses in cheers and good wishes, if not a full hearty meal.

Yes, I know that not all are blessed in such a way, nor that all are able to afford it, or even have family or friends to share it with.

This is the reason I'm writing today, to bring it to the forefront of our minds, as well as implore all of us to make it last.

When it is the season, we can get re-charged, inspired, ignited, and mesmerized thereafter, we can make it a point to remember this specific set of feelings, concentrate within and learn to recognize this set of feelings, so we may be able to re-generate them on demand.

We must never let hurriedness, worries, and the like, stop us from breathing deeply while, remembering the wonderful Light and

Joy experience we have had during the Holidays Season.

If we imagine ourselves to be beacons of Light, bringers of Joy, creators of light-heartedness, continuously throughout the year, imagine how Life may be easier to bear, and many more opportunities to experience love and happiness will be presented to us.

It is not the idea to be 'goo like sweet', or a 'Pollyanna' who could always find the 'silver lining' in everything, it is though, the invitation to exercise our power of choice, prove our independence, as well as our natural innate striving for growth.

By being active beings, who make it a point to be aware and present, who smile fearlessly, help another joyfully, and laugh frequently, we can live better lives, as well as making it easier to all whom we meet to do so too.

When we then take a moment of solitude, aloneness, or even shut our door on the world, we would 'come in' to a place charged with Goodness that will sustain us far better in whatever it is we need to do, or be, by ourselves.

Try it out, see for yourself, and hopefully you'll shine Light and Joy on and on.

Crossing The New Year's Line

We've done it. We crossed the imaginary line from December 31st to January 1st, and we've done it successfully. Well, the Earth is still in one piece, but unfortunately, other non-positive things continue too.

Using the 80/20 percent rule, 80 percent of changes are happening gradually, and only 20 percent happen at once, this is why I would like you to look at the significance we give to New Year's expectations, resolutions, promises, and such.

Our Human nature is a continuous one, our intentions and actions therefore, should be continuous too. Of course, it is wonderful to reach a conclusion (of any kind), and decide to change our intentions and actions from one point onward, but we have to prepare for it otherwise, it will become a failed trial.

Firstly, wake up, look at your life and all the life you effect. Discern if a change is needed, and if yes, check if you're willing to change. Thereafter, check whether you're ready to change, and only then if you have all that it takes to bring the change about.

Change is something we all should be used to, as it is the only constant in life, but this is not to say that everybody welcomes it. Therefore, your own awareness of yourself and what is needed might just make a necessary change more palatable.

My blessing is always: remember to be kind to yourself and others while, very diligently, you keep aware of your life and all that is in it. Do the necessary for growth, empowerment, and remember that happiness is born of simplicity.

What is not managed in this New Year, may be managed any day after it – if you willing to.

Think Small? In A Deed

In this day and age, you hear everywhere that it is best for our success to 'think big' thus, it is so very easy to develop a habit of thinking big in every subject, but is it the right thing to do?

I remember reading Gandhi's biography where he was quoted to say 'be the change you wish to see', and let's add 'in the world', as most of us refer to it in this way.

I would like to draw our attention to the great need for us to think small meaning, close to home, in small matters, in daily life, the life that any action on our behalf will affect someone.

Any one gesture, any one deed carries a ripple effect, which might be subtle, but nevertheless important.

You may actually save someone's life without even knowing it, just by merely influencing their mindset, or their plans.

Unfortunately, the influence may go both in positive and negative directions. Therefore, it is important to pay attention to our intent and direction.

In the aftermath of Haiti 2010 earthquake,

a man decided to 'think small', and take care and supplies to a few orphaned children. Not the whole country and everybody in it, just the few kids. Today, his efforts created a home and a school for sixty kids, who instead of ceasing to exist, are happily brought up despite, their loss of blood family.

One does not need a horrible situation in order to do a good deed, and create goodness. Look around, at home, neighbourhood, community, work, and search for a small good deed you can perform.

Accumulate them, and grow strong, as well as help others around you to grow strong.

Aspires and Inspires

Our innate growth ability and nature, causes us to look for 'increasing' in many ways, in our lives.

It is not a wonder then that both of the words: aspires and inspires are connected to breathing and spirit.

Looking back at your life, as a child, what inspired you? And what did you aspire to be?

Looking at your life now, as an adult, are you still inspired? Have you done anything regarding your childhood aspiration?

I know that the saying: 'it is never too late' might sound as a cliché, but if we've naturally aspired to be authentically aligned, as well as been inspired by what we inwardly known to be aligned with us, is it then ever too late to become better aligned?

There are many reasons why people could not, and are not adhering to their inner 'call'. May it be justified, or not, at least let us not ignore it.

Maybe, just maybe, if we still feed this 'glowing inner coal's' fire by giving it attention, we might find a way, sometime in out days to come, to bring it to light, to express ourselves, as we were meant to, to 'shine' in the truly unique way that is us.

This attention giving could be just an inwardly directed smile at a secret that you only know. You could muse about it, imagine it, write about it, disclose it to a dear friend, and even write a letter to it – as a representative of another magical part of you.

Life's boredom, monotony, and routine, could all be elevated, if we also have a daily acknowledgement of our 'inner call'. I am not talking here about a dream, a dream is something else. Your 'inner call' is real, as much as you are real.

I love talking to people about it, because I always see their eyes starting to shine, their voice quiver a bit, the excitement bubbling under their skin. They become 'alive' and engaging – and I, I wonder how beautifully we were all created, and how much more beauty this world of ours can contain.

Would you dare to lend an ear to yourself and your heart to hear this 'inner call', would you dare to be inspired and to aspire to greatness?

Visual Input Impression and Our Lives

The senses, sight, hearing, and touch, particularly sight, when receiving input from the outside, generate feelings within us. These feelings ignite our thought mechanism, and we find ourselves deep in thoughts flavoured by the input we were just exposed to.

Our life's story is actually woven, as per the flavour and content of our thoughts, so imagine how exposed we really are, and actually how we give our power away while, allowing unguarded input to penetrate us and therefore, our lives.

This is extremely important, specifically in this day and age where, the world is far more connected due to technology, we're far more exposed to what is going on in the world – good or bad (unfortunately, far more bad than good), and in addition we are further exposed to movies and other programs, in the various available media connections.

All this input that most of the times actually does not concern our immediate lives, but life in general, becomes 'extreme noise' whereby, our system is trying to dampen out. When successful, we seem to be nonchalant about life, and when not – we can get sick, or develop other bodily/mind manifestations.

By now you could say – Good Grief...

If this is not enough, consider that our sub-conscious mind doesn't actually differentiate between what is really going on in our lives, and what we're impressed upon by a movie, or watching the evening news.

What are we to do? Surely, we cannot cut ourselves from the world (now that we're all connected), or not have our moments 'away' while watching a favourite program.

While there is a longer list of solutions than space here to discuss, I would like to offer two:

The first is for you to declare to your mind: 'this is just a movie', 'this are somebody else's challenges', and although I can feel for them – 'this is NOT my story or my life'.

The actual declaration sets you apart, and your sub-conscious may take itself now out of gear. This means that you have to be aware and disciplined to do it every day, and every time you're exposed to any non-positive outside impression.

The second solution to consider is monitoring your well-being after your exposure, and making choices to stop watching those things that really have an adverse effect on you.

Let us remember that we can only feel while we live, and we only feel in the present. Isn't it justified for us to feel good most of the times versus not?

If, per chance, you hold a belief that you do not deserve to feel good, please understand that your belief then is in opposition to any law of nature, and look to learn the truth from nature.

If you want to be part of a more peaceful and harmonious world – you have to bring peace into your life, and strive to harmony in all aspects of your life, as well as your thoughts.

I believe that it is possible.

The Zeros In Our Lives

I can hear you say: is there such a thing as a zero in our lives, or do you mean *nothing*?

Well, no, I don't mean 'nothing'. I mean to say that we could look at the concept of a 'zero' in our lives in a different light.

Regardless if you bring forth mathematical, physics, intellectual, or financial arguments, zero actually is 'a state in-between states', it is a thing of value.

Take for example the celebration of birthdays. First, a baby is born, and then we wait for a full year before we celebrate its first year's birthday. We regarded the moment of birth as a start to its life (that we can see, not the nine months of pregnancy). The baby is alive and of presence, it has needs and wants, highs and lows for a full year – and you cannot count that as 'nothing'.

I'd like to offer a view point of looking at zero as an opening, the in-between stage, and definitely a state of value.

Zero came as a great help in counting – carrying us over to the next level, like between 1 and 10, 10 and 100, and so on. It lets us distinguish between one level and another.

The many subjects and methods using a zero are too many to mention here, but what if next time you look at a zero, or think of a zero, you'll have a real look at its shape too.

Zero is marked with O – a circle denoting completion on the one hand, and a re-start on the other. It is also like the letter O for Opening, a doorway to a new space.

Sometimes, I'm sorry to say, people relate to a zero with regards to having nothing in their lives. Mostly because they linger in the in-between state for too long, maybe even because they don't find a way out. This seems like a suspended animation, but who is to say that they're not in a state of hibernation and growth? (Check out my Momentary Thought: 'When a Non-Movement is Hibernation').

It seems to me that it will be much more beneficial to all of us to be more accurate in both our thinking and definitions. Vagueness breeds errors, and really makes us miss the point.

In tongue-and-cheek manner, I would even say (trying not to be too complex) that even the word 'nothing' may be looked at differently. Nothing may become No-Thing, while No may become an acronym for Next One – and here we go again to Next One Thing, which may take us to our next place in life.

May every moment of your lives will be a grand opening to a marvellous greatness.

Impressions

"Emotions, which are feelings in motion, mobilised by the inner sea of vitality and its movements." – TF

Imagine the life force moving in us, similarly to the blood movement in our veins, and then a gust of wind creates waves and ripples that we "feel" thus, the life force difference in motion becomes our emotions.

Therefore, you may ask, what constitutes the gust of wind?

One answer could be "impressions" namely, our whole being gets an impression and affects our life force.

As all is alive and conscious, each and every molecule, there is a constant movement in creation thus, constant changes, which may impress our whole being – impressions that form the gusts of wind.

I started a book called impressions, so many years ago, but never continued with it. I found that the description of the emotions and the experiences that led to them – as a result versus the actual cause, could just have been an exercise in futility.

Somehow, awareness of what is causing certain feelings is much more important, as it directs the person from an outside occurrence, to an inner state that might "entertain" it.

Igniting the inner knowing of one self, following our own responses – calmly and gently, watching ourselves, as we would watch the scenery outside of us, but inwardly – we would find far greater riches and beauty.

I found that movement of body, voice, and mind can create a flow to express those emotions, in dance, song, composition, or writing that may bring a far greater benefit to the person – far more than brewing in the feelings.

This collection of Momentary Thought is one of those expressions in flow.

Creation Like Water

With a thought about cloning and life, I imagined this:

The Godhead and all the sentient beings are like the water. Each drop of water has come from the ocean, and each of these drops will return to the ocean, and on its journey it will nourish the environment, and sustain life, which is the mirror of Creation.

The Godhead is the whole. Each one of us is just a mere drop within the Godhead. When Light is thrown upon us – Creation can be seen.

Whether we are to create another sentient being, or an artificial entity, we are utilising the Living Waters and Light to do so. Thus, we open the opportunity for the Godhead to bless it, and either to grant it a soul, or not. The Godhead is the only one who grants souls, whether we acknowledge the existence of souls, or not. This is the reason why it is so dangerous, because those of our creations who are able to affect lives, and which were not blessed with a soul, will not have the innate–consciousness to discern between Right and Wrong, and follow the Divine path of love, harmony, and compassion, and thus may bring havoc to life. One example is within the cells of our bodies, each may be striving for health for the whole organism, or only for their own and thus, lead to disease, such as cancer.

Therefore, we, just like the drops of water, have to be aware of, and acknowledge, our innate gift of life and its attributes, and follow its *theme* and thus, we will follow our destiny, and fulfill our lives' purposes.

Give life: let live and live yourself.

A word about this series

In this busy day and age, where people have more input than they sometimes able to concentrate on, I venture to offer a more succinct manner of dealing with subjects of interest, or need.

The image of a tip of an iceberg immediately brings to mind that there is much more unseen, underwater if you may.

Consciousness is very much like the waters of a vast sea whereby, our conscious thoughts are those that exist above the water level, and our submerged portion of the conscious – is very much our unknown part therefore, many times it is called the sub-conscious, or the unconscious.

Our feelings are just the waves, and wave crests, which are created by the winds of time, and occurrences of life upon the surface.

I'd like to have your brief time of contemplation in reading this short book yet, to impress your mind with a profound message, and content.

It is in the succinct that we may never be overwhelmed, and in overpowering vast amount of input that we are fatigued.

Momentary Thoughts

I trust you know that much more could have been said about the subject of the book, but maybe what was said is enough.

I wish you joy and peace – always.

Notes

Notes

Notes

Notes

Notes

Notes

www.ingramcontent.com/pod-product-compliance
Lightning Source LLC
Chambersburg PA
CBHW031407160426
43196CB00007B/930